Under-Fives in the Infant Classroom

Christine Pascal

Trentham Books

© Christine Pascal 1990

First published in 1990 by
Trentham Books Ltd.,
Unit 13/14,
Trent Trading Park,
Botteslow Street,
Hanley,
Stoke-on-Trent, Staffs ST1 3LY.

ISBN 0 948080 41 8

Set and printed in Great Britain by:
The Bemrose Press Ltd., Chester.

British Library Cataloguing in Publication Data
Pascal, Christine
Under-fives in the infant classroom.
1. England. Primary schools. Teaching methods
I. Title
372.130942

ISBN 0-948080-41-8   **Price £3.95**

Under-Fives in the Infant Classroom

Transplanting children from home to school is very like transplanting seed-
lings from a seed tray out into the garden: timing is crucial and conditions
must be right for them to grow ahead without any setbacks. Transplant
them too early and they'll take a long time to get going again; transplant
them too late and they may become "pot-bound" — too set in their ways
to branch out satisfactorily.

Easing the Transition from Home to School PPA (1983)

Many adults can recall something of that first experience of school — be
it the smell of warm milk, the image of large shiny floors, a caring or
thoughtless remark, the jangle of the piano, the fear of parting from a secure
adult — these memories remain with us and may still affect our behaviour
many years later. It is interesting that often what is recalled is not *what* was
taught but *how* it was taught. The context and the interactions within it are
critical in the learning that goes on.

Longitudinal studies of the effect of early childhood programmes on subse-
quent development provide evidence of the importance of a child's first en-
counters with formal schooling (Schweinhart et al 1986, Osborn and Milbank
1987, Tizard et al 1988). Alongside, there is mounting evidence that starting
school is a potentially stressful time for young children (Cleave et al 1982,
Barrett 1986, Pascal and Ghaye 1988). Set in this context the increasing trend
to admit young children into formal schooling with little consideration of
the implications of this in terms of policy, provision and practice needs careful
scrutiny. There are currently a number of factors which add urgency to this
need.

Firstly, there is a growing trend towards a policy of annual admission into
school in the year in which children become five (Cleave et al 1985, Woodhead
1989). Also, many local authorities are admitting 'rising fives' on a termly
basis. Current figures show that as many as 62% of four year olds are in
infant classes (HMI 1989). Studies have shown that these young children can
be under some stress in the school situation and this is compounded by a
lack of appropriate facilities and, often, an inappropriate curriculum (HMI
1989, Pascal 1989, Bennett and Kell 1989). The change in admission policy

1

is the result of a number of factors, falling school rolls, parental demand for early educational provision, demographic and economic trends and research which has shown the disadvantages accruing to summer-born children under termly entry arrangements, being amongst these (Woodhead 1989). The indications are that this pattern of admission will become more common and the change is a significant one, breaking with long established conventions about the kind of educational environment which is appropriate at school level and earlier. This places a great responsibility on those involved in developing admission policies and those teaching these young children to re-examine their provision and practice to ensure they are meeting the developmental needs of the children in their care.

A second, and linked factor, is the increasing shortage of teaching staff, especially those qualified to teach under-fives in schools, coupled with a shortage of local advisers with experience to support them and tutors with the appropriate expertise to train them. Concern has been voiced about this situation for some time following the publication of surveys which have shown as few as 10% of primary teachers with nursery/infant training (TES 9/9/88). The case for in-depth training which is academically rigorous and of high quality at initial and in-service level for teachers involved with our youngest children must be advocated strongly. This is particularly important at a time of acute shortage when strategies such as the redeployment of teachers from surplus areas and the appointment of licensed and articled teachers are being seriously considered by schools as ways in which shortages may be quickly met.

A third factor is the passing of the Education Reform Act. The implications of this act are enormous and the introduction of the national curriculum, assessment and testing will affect everyone in the system. However, it has especially worrying implications for those involved with under-fives in the school system who are already subject to downward pressures to adopt a more formal, subject-based curriculum for these children. Statements from the National Curriculum Council have so far done little to reassure these teachers.

Yet there are positive signs, The White Paper *Better Schools* (1985) had pointed to the dangers of introducing young children too early to formal work. This was echoed in the Select Committee Report, *Achievement in Primary Schools* (1986) which acknowledged the move towards annual admission of children into infant schools but asserted that this should only be accepted where the curriculum and provision was comparable with those in nursery schools and classes. The more recent report of the Education, Science and Arts Committee, *Educational Provision for the Under Fives* (1988) added support to this and recommended that:

> No further steps should be taken by LEAs towards introducing 3 and 4 year olds into inappropriate primary school settings. Policies in LEAs of annual (September) entry of 4 year olds into school should be explicitly subject to the availability of appropriate provision and should normally

be for part-time places (22,7.13).

Further steps should be taken (possibly encouraged by an ESG) by those LEAs with four-year-olds in their reception classes to bring all their reception classes up to the required standard, in particular to establish an appropriate staffing ratio (24,7.15).

The Government response to this has been to establish a Committee of Inquiry, chaired by the Minister of State at the DES, to consider the quality and content of the educational experience offered to under-fives. This committee is due to report in January 1990 and it is hoped that some positive action with regard to policy and provision for four year olds in reception classes will follow.

In short, the policy of admitting four year olds into school is being given a high profile and concerns about it are being voiced and felt at a number of levels. If we are to achieve the best for these children and ensure that an early start to school is advantageous to them, rather than detrimental, careful scrutiny of what is happening in schools as a result of early admission policies is a priority. At present studies have tended to be quantitative in their approach, focusing on the facts and figures of admission policies and levels of provision within and between LEAs and different countries. There is an urgent need for detailed information about the quality of provision and practice relating to under-fives in school and how the classroom process affects pre-statutory age children. The purpose of this project was therefore to investigate the quality of the experience offered to four year olds in reception classes within one local authority.

The findings presented in this report form the second part of a two year research project looking at the experience of being at school before statutory schooling age. Part one of the study had focused on the experience of starting school at four. It examined in some detail the feelings, expectations, understandings and perceptions of children, parents and teachers involved in the admission process. It became clear from this study that starting school at four was potentially very stressful, particularly where school policy, provision and practice did not take into account the developmental needs of these younger children (Pascal and Ghaye 1988). Part two of the study followed these children through their first year in school and focused on what was being offered to them: What was the context, materially and interpersonally, into which they were being admitted and what did the curriculum consist of? Two schools were studied in depth, the researcher working alongside the teacher for a day a week throughout the year. In addition, a questionnaire was sent to every LEA maintained mainstream reception class with four year olds in the authority, (193 in total), in order to gain a broad sweep of policy and practice. It was hoped that this would provide a picture of what was actually happening in schools where a policy of early admission was accepted practice.

Data was gathered in four main areas:

1. The type of school, its admission policies, the size and age range of the class.
2. The training and experience of the class teacher, the availability and use of ancillary support, the extent of parental involvement.
3. The management and organisation of the space, facilities and equipment available.
4. The curriculum provided and teaching/learning strategies employed.

The data cannot claim to be representative of all reception classes containing four year olds. For example, there were few small schools of the type which predominate in the shire counties with their particular problems of vertically grouped classes, nor were there any special schools or voluntary aided schools in the sample. However, the findings presented are based on the self reported practice of 135 reception class teachers, and the researcher's own observations and experiences in two city schools over a year. The quality of the responses received is indicative of the concern felt by those teaching these young children in school and they stand as an example of practice and provision in a large metropolitan authority which had had four years experience of annual admission policies. The LEA had adopted a policy of annual admission to school in 1984. There had been some increase in capitation and ancillary help to support this. Since then there had been a gradual increase in in-service opportunities for reception class teachers but this was still small scale at the time of the study and many teachers had not benefited from this. There were general LEA guidelines for an early years curriculum but no written guidance specifically aimed to help teachers of four years olds.

Admission policies
The 135 schools in the study admitting four year olds were organised on an infant, infant/junior or primary basis (see Table 1).

Table 1: Type of school

Type of school	% schools
Infant school with a nursery on site	16%
Infant school with no nursery on site	21%
Junior/Infant school with a nursery on site	27%
Junior/Infant school with no nursery on site	36%

Almost two out of three of the reception classes were in J/I or primary schools, while one out of three were in infant schools. Nursery provision in the LEA was quite high, with more than 40% of these schools having a nursery on site. Evidence from parents and teachers revealed that often four year olds were taken out of a nursery school or class to join the reception class. Nursery teachers expressed great concern about this. The links between the pre-school providers and the schools were very variable: in cases where provision was all on one site communication was easy and usually well developed, in others it was non-existent. There was some evidence that the reception classes in large J/I and primary schools were the least well provided for, having to compete for resources against the rest of the school priorities and often headed by an unsympathetic male head with little or no early years experience. The status and gender of reception class teachers undoubtedly contributed to this situation.

Virtually all of the schools (98%) had an annual intake, which was usually staggered over a few days, and attendance in 78% of schools was full time from the start (Table 2).

Table 2: Admission procedures

Intake policy	% schools
Annual intake	98%
Termly intake	2%
Full time	78%
Part time	22%

Although many class teachers expressed a wish for part time attendance, at least initially, pressure from parents was seen as a limiting factor. Of the 22% of schools which did have part time attendance, this varied from periods of a few days to half a term, with very few schools stating that transfer to full time attendance was flexible and determined by the needs of the children. This situation contrasts sharply with the line taken in recent HMI and Government reports and teachers were clearly anxious about the effect this pattern of admission had on the children. As one teacher commented,

> We must recognise and cater for the very special needs of these young children. They should not be forced into a system that is often not equipped to deal with them. The transition must be gradual and tailored to their individual needs.

Induction policies were variable, most schools having some form of pre-admission visit(s) to school but only one school mentioned the use of home visits before entry.

The size of the classes to which the children were admitted raises a number of issues. Although there is much evidence that under-fives do not function well in large groups and need the security and stimulus of relationships found only with small numbers, 40% of the reception classes in the study were over 30 and only 10% were less than 20 (see Table 3). This is almost double the number typically found in nursery classes (DES 1987) and compares poorly with the non-statutory recommendation of the Select Committee that 26 should be the maximum size for classes admitting four year olds.

The paucity of this situation is compounded further by the staffing ratios which were nowhere near that found in nursery provision. Further, two thirds of the reception classes had a 12 month or more age range within them, the result of placing all the children from one year of entry together. Only one third of schools divided off the pre-statutory age children from the statutory

Table 3: Size of class and age range

Class size	% classes
15-20	10%
21-25	22%
26-30	28%
31-35	40%
Age range in classes	
4.1-4.8	36%
4.1-5.8	62%
4.1-7.1	2%

age starters. There were conflicting views expressed on the desirability of mixing the annual intake or keeping the younger ones separate but issues were raised about the differentiation of provision, given the wide developmental range in the mixed entrance classes.

The teachers were well aware of the difficulties caused by admission policies and comments like these reflect their concerns:

'I feel strongly that such pupils should not attend full time primary school in such large classes as they require the more informal education of the nursery and then they should only attend full time as a gradual process, not an overnight separation from home. This would help those in the reception class to be more responsive and show less signs of restlessness, boredom, lack of concentration and often bad behaviour — all symptoms related to a basic lack of understanding of what is going on.'

'With limited space and only one teacher, 30 four to five year olds is too many and more than 30 is ridiculous.'

'The main issue is class size. The four year old needs the opportunity to talk about his (sic) play and work so he can benefit to the full.'

'Four year old children need to feel safe and secure, so much smaller classes or groups would be less daunting for them.'

Staffing

Given the increasing lack of trained and experienced early years practitioners at all levels it is not surprising that the staffing of the reception classes in the study raises some issues of grave concern. Table 4 shows the percentage distribution of teachers in the survey in the age ranges of their initial teacher training.

Table 4: Teacher's Training

Age range trained for	% Teachers
3- 5	0%
3- 7	12%
5- 7	48%
7-11	23%
8-13	7%
11-16	2%
11-18	8%

four out of 10 teachers of four year olds had no specific early years training and 10% had not even primary training, coming from a middle or secondary trained background (see Table 4). Indeed, there were nearly as many middle/secondary trained teachers as nursery trained teachers taking these reception classes. The teachers did, however, tend to be experienced practitioners, indicating that heads often put their older, more experienced teachers in these classes (see Table 5).

Yet coupled with the paucity of in-service opportunities, this means that, even for those with appropriate training, training was out of date and not specifically geared to the special needs of under-fives in infant schools. Teachers were often well aware of this,

'I believe more specific training should be given for those teaching reception age children.'

'I feel very strongly that this age group requires a very experienced infant trained teacher with tremendous energy and enthusiasm.'

8

Table 5: Teacher Experience

Years of infant experience	% teachers
0-5	11%
5-10	36%
10 +	53%

It was also interesting to note that only 6% of the reception class teachers had any sort of senior management responsibilities within the school (see Table 6).

Table 6: Management Responsibility of Reception Class Teachers

Area of management responsibility	% teachers
Reception class only	48%
Reception class + curriculum area/year group	46%
Head/deputy head of infants	6%

This raises all sorts of questions about the status and career structure for teachers assuming responsibility for these classes, as well as their access to and influence upon policy decisions within the school. Teachers in the reception classes tended to be experienced practitioners but lacking in career advancement. This might be the result of either headteachers placing teachers with little career ambition in these classes or of a career block for those teachers taking responsibility for reception classes. The whole issue of career patterns of those teaching young children needs further investigation.

As had been stated, reception classes tended to be large, but nearly all of them had some measure of ancillary support (see Table 7). Schools had been given an allowance for this when the LEA had introduced the policy of annual admission and this compares favourably with those LEAs admitting four year olds without any ancillary provision . . . However, in practice this support was generally not full time and in only 34% of cases was the ancillary trained.

Table 7: Ancillary Support

Level of support	% classes
Classes with support	99%
Classes without support	1%
Full Time	27%
More than half time	51%
Less than half time	22%
Trained	34%
Untrained	66%

In many instances, therefore, teachers were found to be coping single-handed with a large class of four year olds. The teachers argued unanimously that trained, full time ancillary help was the most vital ingredient for effective teaching:

'Sufficient ancillary support is required to ensure the quality of education offered is the best available.'

'A full time classroom assistant is essential.'

'The skills acquired during the early years are very important as building blocks for later life, particularly language. In order that children acquire these skills in an enjoyable and caring environment, there should be two adults to thirty children at all times. Much of the learning at this stage will be through doing and talking and staffing should reflect this.'

These views are supported strongly by the Select Committee recommendation that:

there should be a full time anciallary worker in addition to the teacher if the full time equivalent of the number of four year olds at the beginning of the term exceeds 6. It is desirable that the ancillary worker should have the qualifications of the NNEB. (5.45)

Teachers also expressed frustration at the fact that at the time of the study ancillary staff were excluded from the in-service training provided for teachers of four year olds.

The extent of parental involvement within the school and classroom was also variable. Despite the research evidence which has underlined the importance of establishing a collaborative partnership with parents in these early years, over 40% of teachers in the study did not encourage this to the extent of involving parents in their classroom (see Table 8).

Table 8: Parental Involvement in Classrooms

Parental involvement	% classes
Yes	60%
No	40%

Many reasons were stated to justify this position e.g. lack of interest, cultural and economic barriers, the threat to teachers' professionality, confidentiality, management and time problems. Few schools appeared to have a written policy on parent links which would give support and consistency, and guide the teachers and other staff. Also, few teachers had ever received any training in the skills required to manage this effectively.

Those schools where parents were actively involved indicated the benefits which accrued from this. Generally, these were seen as providing an extra pair of hands, another adult to interact with the children and an important source of information about the children. Although the value of these parental contributions must not be under-estimated and teachers generally were very positive about the benefits, few pointed to the unique and significant contribution parents could make to the collaborative venture of teaching the children. The various roles assumed by parents in the study schools are summarised below:

1. School-based activities

— cutting paper
— mounting work
— typing
— making books
— making coffee at meetings
— library
— bookshop

2. Classroom-based activities

— talking
— helping run pre-school groups
— cooking
— school trips
— swimming
— games
— hearing readers
— art and craft

One teacher summed up the feeling expressed by many others:

'We should not have to rely on the goodwill of parents to provide essential help. Parental help should be an additional bonus, not a necessity.'

This view encapsulates the philosophy that parents are seen as second rate ancillary support and not as an essential and vital partner in the process of educating these four year olds.

Resourcing and Facilities

The level of resource provision in the reception classes was very variable. This includes not only equipment and facilities but also the organisation of the learning context in which these children were being taught. There is much supporting evidence from other LEAs that the lack of adequate resources is a widespread difficulty faced by teachers of four year olds (Thomas 1987, Peel 1988). One of the reasons for this is that LEAs do not have to provide capitation for these pre-statutory age children. The LEA in which the study took place had allocated small amounts to schools for this but even then the findings paint a picture of often poorly resourced classrooms and inappropriate organisation of existing resources.

When teachers were asked what they felt to be essentials, after full time ancillary help, appropriate equipment (particularly large play equipment), more space, adjoining toilet and washing facilities and access to an outdoor area were rated as most important (see Table 9). It is interesting to note that these are all minimum requirements for nursery schools and classes.

Many classrooms did not have these essentials; less than 1 in 3 classrooms had adjoining toilets, only 1 in 3 had access to an outside area and 4 out of 10 did not have a sink within them at all (see Table 10).

Space was seen to be at a premium, with many teachers bemoaning the cramped feeling in their rooms which was the result of trying to provide as many experiences as possible in too small an area with too many children.

Teachers were asked to draw a layout of their classrooms and outline the rationale behind it. These plans and accompanying explanations provide a

13

Table 9: Resources seen as essential by teachers

Essential resources	% teachers
Trained full time ancillary support	97%
Appropriate equipment for inside/outside	74%
Space	52%
Adjoining toilets/washing facilities	27%
Access to outdoor areas	7%
Appropriately trained teacher	6%
Range of picture bocks	6%
Sink with h/c water	2%

Table 10: Classes without essential resources

Essential resources	% classes
Adjoining toilets	71%
Access to outdoor area	67%
Sink with h/c water	43%

a fascinating insight into the philosophies of these teachers and the experiences they offered children within the learning contexts they had planned. A small sample of these have been reproduced (Figs. 1-6) as an illustration of the wide range of practice and provision demonstrated.

Figure 1: Classroom Layout of Teacher A

'The organisation of my room is changed frequently to suit our requirements. The carpet area is used for floor toys, construction, story and playhouse. The wet area is for natural materials play and creative work. The dry area is used for skills/number work, table top toys, dough etc . . .'

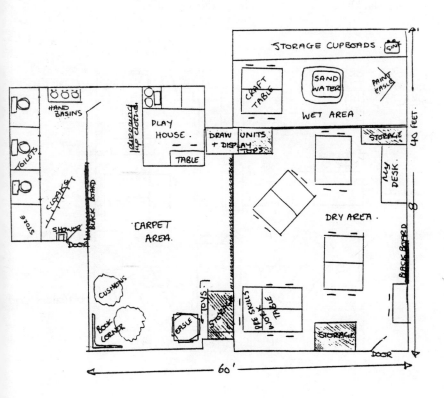

Figure 2: Classroom Layout of Teacher B

'Due to great limitations of room, mainly size, cupboards are used for display and as a teacher base rather than a conventional teacher's desk. As much space as possible has been created for greater movement of children, (chairs have to remain tucked under tables for greater space). Tables are rearranged when the blackboard is in use e.g. letter formation exercises, so that all children are facing towards the teacher. Most desks are already situated close to the blackboard and require little adjustment.'

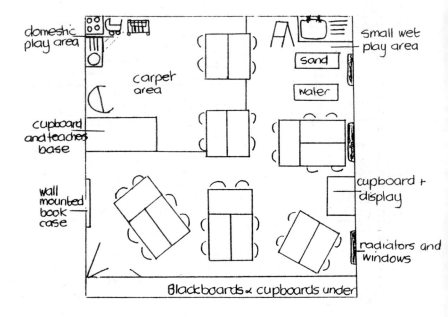

Figure 3: Classroom Layout of Teacher C

'Space is so limited and the three doors, all heavily used and being where they are, mean it is very difficult to make provision for 30 children and necessary activity areas. The placing of children's desks is governed by sight of the blackboard. Water play is only possible when the glass doors can be opened and the terrace used. Large toys can also be used outdoors in good weather.'

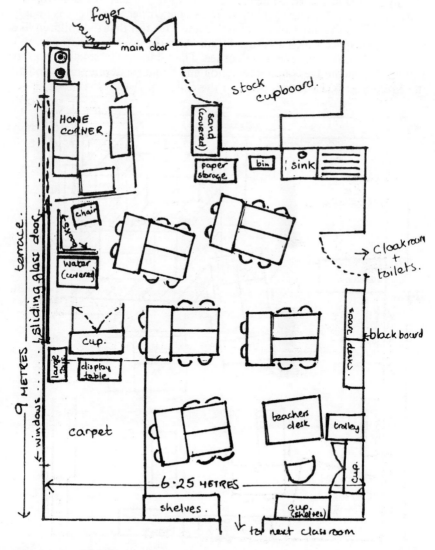

Figure 4: Classroom Layout of Teacher D

'The wet area of the classroom is obviously already set and this is where the majority of the messy art work is completed. The water play, sand play and plasticene table are situated in this area as it is easier to clean being uncarpeted. The quiet area is positioned in the top corner because less noise seems to penetrate from other classrooms than in the bottom corner of the class. I use my desk and the equipment trolley to form an enclosed area for the children to sit in for class activities. The home corner is where it is mainly because that is the only corner available and I do feel that the children like the enclosed space which a corner offers. Also the noise stimulated by this area is well away from the quiet corner. The tables are in small groups as I think this encourages pupil interaction and language development and all the equipment is easily accessible to the children.'

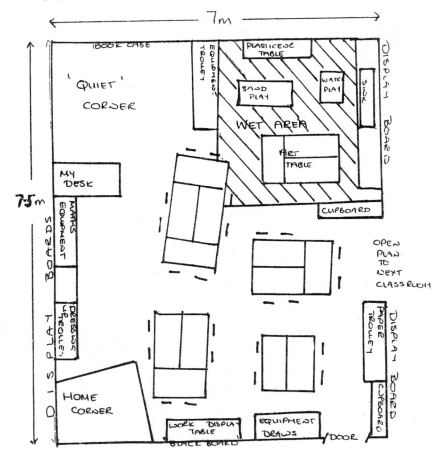

Figure 5: Classroom Layout of Teacher E

'The room is organised in this way so that children may move from area to area, (sometimes freely, sometimes under my direction), to participate in a wide range of activities during any one session. By this arrangement I aim to maximise my use of space and resources.'

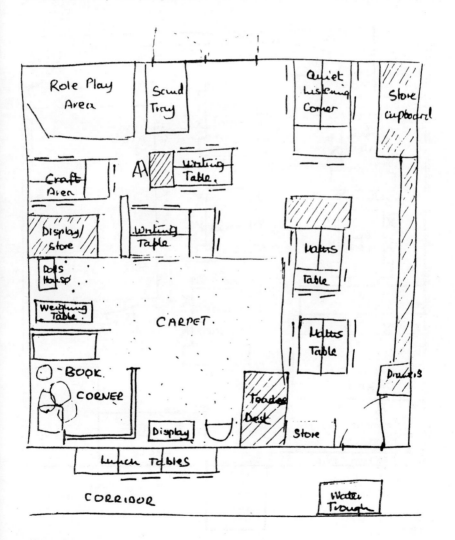

Figure 6: Classroom Layout of Teacher F

'The room is organised in this way to give the maximum amount of space. All children can see the blackboard when necessary. The mat is situated where the children can sit to read books and is also used for a play area with large toys. There is very little space for the sand tray and no space for water play in the classroom.'

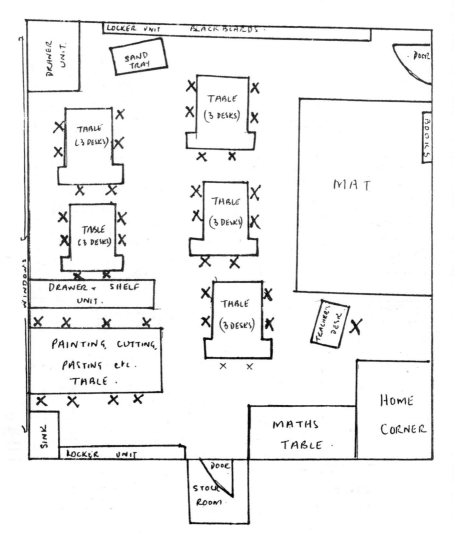

Table 11 summarises the facilities that were available in the reception classrooms.

Table 11: Facilities available in reception classrooms

Facilities	% classrooms
Domestic play area	81%
Wet play area	62%
Quiet/book area	60%
Open/active play area	6%
Carpeted area	88%
Work/table area	87%
Outside play area	33%
Sand play	68%
Water play	53%

Eight out of 10 classrooms had some form of domestic play area but this tended to be fixed and static. A few teachers indicated a flexible arrangement which they adapted to a variety of play themes e.g. a hospital, a shop, a spaceship, a garage but this was the exception and domestic play predominated in this area of provision. Six out of 10 classrooms had sand play and five out of 10 had water play. Teachers expressed difficulties about such things as lack of space, suitable floor coverings, lack of supervision beacuse they were located in corridors and caretaker troubles. Given that these are nursery age children, the lack of basic materials play is very worrying and reflects the emphasis on more formal table-based activities. Only one in three classrooms had direct access to an outside area with large toys suitable for outdoor play and many teachers expressed anxiety that this kind of gross motor activity was often missing from their daily routine because of this. Having facilities for wet or messy play was linked to these restrictions and over four out of 10 classrooms had no sink and no clearly defined wet play area within the classroom. Nearly nine out of 10 classrooms had a carpeted area which was seen as a base and a very important meeting point for the children and staff. This often doubled up as the quiet area serving a variety of purposes, a discussion point, a teaching base, a book and reading area, a rest area and a floor play area and teachers pointed to difficulties caused by the competing functional demands of these. There were very few examples of classrooms having totally separate quiet areas where the children could go to rest or just do something in an atmosphere of peace and tranquility.

The teachers rationales revealed that generally they tried to create the following areas in their rooms:

a wet/messy area

a quiet area

an active play area

a work area.

However, many argued that lack of space put severe restrictions on this and meant that they had to make difficult decisions about how to balance the space available between these areas. The compromises that teachers had made were revealed in their classroom plans and reflect clearly the teachers' priorities when making these choices. The teachers' rationales support this view and demonstrate how the physical environment shapes and influences the curriculum that takes place within it. In a significant number of cases the areas of activity were forced to overlap and some got subsumed altogether. For example, the quiet area was often the floor construction area, the messy area was often the active play area or the messy area often disappeared out of the classroom altogether.

Given the cramped feeling of many of the classrooms and the lack of sufficient space for play activities, it was very significant that in nearly nine out of 10 classrooms tables and chairs predominated in the space available. There was generally a desk and chair provided for every child and these were centrally placed. All other facilities and equipment were arranged *around* these. The arrangement of the tables and chairs thus dictated the room layout and gave the impression in a majority of cases of a very formal and deskbound environment. Space was often so tight around these that it was hard for the children and staff to squeeze between them to reach the other activity areas. Very few classrooms had any space left for an open area where children could move around freely or try out large motor skills (and this generally in classrooms with no access to an outdoor area).

There were examples of small classrooms with large numbers of children being organised imaginatively and successfully to create an appropriate environment for these young children. In these classrooms teachers had created small areas whithin which children could converse, develop group strategies and work imaginatively and with concentration on the task in hand. Space was provided for floor activities and for children to move around easily. The use of low screens, display boards and cupboards created an interesting and varied environment in which equipment was accessible to the children at the appropriate height and in suitably labelled and tidy containers. Yet in many classrooms this was not the case. The frustration of some of the teachers was evident in the comments below but often teachers were not aware that what they were providing was a learning context geared to suit children much older than four.

'I have just moved with a group of children from the nursery class to the reception class and the difference was so dramatic. Gone was the wonderful space, the large apparatus, jigsaws, construction toys, purpose built toilets, purpose built outside apparatus and, of course, the 1:13 ratio. I felt frustrated and disappointed — can you imagine how the children felt?'

'Children who have previously experienced a nursery education are used to working in quiet, messy or play areas which are all isolated beautifully in most nursery schools. We are expected to cater for all these needs in an ordinary classroom and I do not feel that the child's needs can be satisfied fully when they still need room to play imaginatively and yet are expected to develop more refined learning skills.'

Curriculum Content and Delivery

The teachers in the study were asked what were their priorities in planning the curriculum for four year olds. Table 12 reveals the rank order of the curriculum priorities for the teachers.

Table 12: Teachers' Expressed Curriculum Priorities

Activities	% Teachers choosing
Free/Imaginative Play	82%
Spoken Language	69%
Early Numeracy	61%
Creative Artwork	54%
Early Reading	53%
Written Language	43%
Gross Motor Skills	42%
Natural Materials Play	39%
Fine Motor Skills	37%
Construction Play	27%
Music/Singing	19%
Social Discipline	12%
Science	6%
Computers	1%
Exploring Outside Environment	1%

The table shows what the teachers *said* were their curriculum priorities. Notably, play and talk were well above the more formal subject based activities. Also interestingly, science and computer skills figured very low in their priorities. This table becomes significant when compared against the information the teachers provided outlining how they organised and delivered this curriculum to the children and points to an anomaly between what teachers purport and what they practice. This data can be categorised as falling roughly into three main types of delivery:

1. TRADITIONAL SPLIT — which can be characterised as 'work in the mornings, play in the afternoons'

2. TRADITIONAL FORMAL — which can be characterised as highly structured formal activities, 'we always play on Friday afternoons'

3. PROGRESSIVE INTEGRATED — which can be characterised as a blend of structured and unstructured activities in which work and play cannot be distinguished, 'there is no division between work and play'

Clearly, these are broad stereotypical categorisations of the range of teaching approaches adopted in the classrooms studied. However, there was a surprising degree of uniformity to the patterns of the day that many teachers operated and this gives the analysis a descriptive validity. Table 13 shows the proportion of teachers adopting these types of approach to deliver their curriculum.

Table 13: Types of Curriculum Delivery

Curriculum approach	% teachers using
Traditional split	62%
Traditional formal	6%
Progressive integrated	31%

1. Traditional Split
More than six out of 10 teachers appeared to adopt the Traditional Split approach to deliver their curriculum. Accounts of a typical day in the

classroom revealed a high degree of consistency of practice between teachers adopting this style of delivery. Generally, the children came in and met on the carpeted area for registration, which was often followed by assembly. Following this would be a short teacher led discussion which had various names, 'chat time', 'mat time', 'together time', and was seen as an important part of the teaching process. It was here that the morning's activities were outlined and new concepts, skills or knowledge were introduced. The children were then usually split into groups for either language or number work. This morning period tended to be table based, the children working with a teacher or ancillary. These groups rotated during the morning with a break for drinks and playtime. After lunch the children would meet again on the mat and the afternoon's activities would be explained. These tended to be less formal, more active play activities and often an element of choice was given to the children. Following afternoon playtime stories, singing and poetry ended the day. P.E. and TV timetable slots would be fitted into this programme throughout the week.

2. Traditional Formal

Less than one in 10 teachers appeared to adopt the Traditional Formal approach but this reveals its continued existence in classrooms with four year olds. Typically, the whole day was very tightly structured and formally organised. The children came in for registration and then the morning was broken up into number, language and writing sessions. Sometimes these were whole class sessions, sometimes the work was done in ability groups. The activities in the main were table based, with a break for morning play. After lunch the activities offered ranged from topic or project work, art and craft, P.E. or TV with teachers directing all these activities. Play was not given formal time allocation or acknowledgement in the organisation of the day, except as something the children could do when they had finished their work. The day usually finished with a story, poetry or singing.

3. Progressive Integrated

Three out of 10 teachers appeared to adopt the Progressive Integrated approach. Their accounts of a typical day generally included the following features. The children would come in and meet on the mat for registration and a discussion time; again this was seen as an important feature of the day. During this time a range of activities would be explained to the children. These would typically involve experience across the curriculum, often one activity combining these in a very practical way e.g. sand and water activity might involve some scientific problem solving, some maths and some language work. Children were sometimes offered an element of choice, either totally free or structured e.g. they might be given two or three tasks to complete during the morning at their own pace, but often they were allocated to groups and rotated. The teacher and ancillary tended to be based at what were termed 'high guidance' activities where some direct teaching might go on. The morning was usually split by drinks and playtime. After the lunch the format was similar but with much more choice and freedom of movement allowed. Again, after afternoon play the day finished with stories or singing. P.E. and TV were slotted into the pattern when timetabled.

The study also investigated what teaching strategies were adopted and Table 14 summarises the results:

Table 14: Teaching Strategies Employed

Teaching strategies	% Teachers using
teacher directed/whole class e.g. story, letter formation	97%
teacher directed/group e.g. language, maths activities	99%
teacher directed/individual e.g. reading, writing activities	98%
child directed/individual e.g. creative art, free play	83%
child directed/group e.g. creative activities, construction play	78%
child directed/whole class e.g. drama, singing, story	53%

From this table it can be seen that virtually all the teachers used a range of teacher directed strategies, from whole class to individuals, but were less comfortable with child directed strategies, except on an individual or sometimes group base and with less formal activities. Nearly half the teachers did not provide children with the opportunity or experience of leading and initiating an activity for the whole class, and many not even for a group. Teachers' comments revealed that they felt they should be in control, particularly in formal 3R's work. This finding raises important questions about the encouragement of children to be independent, autonomous, self disciplined learners. Giving children responsibility for their learning was not a widespread practice.

From this analysis of the teachers' accounts of how they delivered their curriculum, it is evident that there is a considerable mismatch between what teachers say and what teachers do. Although teachers had stressed free, imaginative play and talk as being priorities in their curriculum, their delivery did not reflect this. The priority was on the more formal 3R's work and teachers' time was predominantly spent supporting these activities. Teachers generally spent little time 'playing' alongside the children and adult support here, where it existed, was left to ancillaries and parents. Most teachers did claim to organise the children on a group basis but the children observed were often working within these groups on an individual basis, particularly in the more formal areas of language and maths. There was little evidence of children collaborating to problem solve except in activities such as construction play.

A number of points emerge from this analysis of how the children experience the curriculum on offer:

1. 'Mat time' was seen as a central part of the social and teaching process in virtually all the classrooms.

2. Story time was another consistent feature and generally took place at the end of the day.

3. Few teachers spent time 'playing' alongside the children, this was left to support staff.

4. Most of the teaching was done in groups with teachers directing the activity.

5. Managing to hear the children read was mentioned as a continual pressure on teaching staff.

6. Parents were rarely mentioned as part of the teaching team.

7. Little time was given to encourage children to recall and review the activities they had undertaken.

8. Teachers, and therefore children, saw a clear division between work and play activities.

9. Teachers found it hard to cater for the wide range of abilities and experiences of the children and to differentiate the curriculum accordingly.

Many teachers did express concern about the inappropriateness of the infant curriculum they offered to these four year old children but few had successfully modified their practice. They felt there were a variety of pressures from colleagues, parents and others. Some teachers acknowledged the need to develop their practice but were limited by their own admitted lack of knowledge and experience. The 1985 White Paper, *Better Schools,* had stated,

> Very young children can be introduced too early to the more formal language and number skills and they miss essential exploratory and practical work through which a good nursery provision forms a sound basis for better learning.

Yet despite this and other strong supportive official statements about the inappropriateness of a formal curriculum for these children, many teachers still felt under great pressure to use formal methods, particularly with the introduction of the National Curriculum:

> 'I feel strongly that if four year olds are to be admitted into infant schools they should not be full time and it should be made clear to parents that a nursery curriculum is to be followed and that early entry does not mean early access to an academic curriculum.'

> 'Catering for large numbers of four year olds is a difficult challenge without extra help, more resources and some guidelines. I am particularly worried that the new National Curriculum could be applied to four year olds in classes for children of compulsory school age. A National Curriculum involving targets, directed study and testing could be unsuitable and potentially damaging to the education of under fives.'

> 'It is important to remember that these children are not "reception children" as we know them and play is still very important. Most teachers seem to be too eager to start formal reading and number work too early.'

'Whilst many children aged four are capable of commencing formal education, some do seem very young and providing different activities for very young children whilst others are concentrating on very basic work is difficult. I feel the whole question of proper education for very young children needs to be examined.

'There is a need to protect four year olds from formal school routines and assemblies, playtimes and formal work. Value should be given to play and child initiated learning.'

'Expect the most of them — they'll give it to you. Mine are already using dictionaries and have made a tape slide.'

'I would like to feel there was a higher parental awareness of the importance of the whole range of curriculum activities in this year. Despite great efforts at our school to inform parents about approaches to reading and maths, the expectation is still that a four year old will be taught to read and taught sums in the first term in school and that they are failing if this is not achieved. I find it very stressful to reconcile my own fairly informed judgements about what is important at this stage educationally with the expectations and desires of parents who have a genuine concern for the education of their children.'

Conclusion

Finally, teachers were asked to reflect upon provision for the four year olds in their care and to indicate areas in which support would help them to improve the quality of the educational experience they offered. Table 15 provides a rank order of expressed need of the 135 reception teachers in the study and reveals what their priorities are. There was a considerable degree of consensus amongst the teachers on what they needed to improve the quality of their provision and practice. The list provides clear guidance for action for those developing and implementing policy decisions in this area.

These all have high resource implications but as one teacher pointed out,

'Quality provision will inevitably cost more.'

In conclusion, the evidence presented in this report raises a number of important issues for those concerned with the quality of the educational experience offered to four year olds in schools:

1. The quality of the provision is very much dependent on the *quality of those who staff* these classes. At present they often lack appropriate training and many still have not had the opportunity to undertake any inservice, although this is now a national priority.

2. There is much concern about the *poor adult/child ratio* in many of these reception classes, given the particular need of these young children to have plenty of opportunities for substantial and meaningful dialogue with an adult.

Table 15: Expressed Needs of Reception Class Teachers

1. Full time trained ancillary support

2. Inservice training

3. Appropriate facilities and equipment

4. Smaller classes

5. Specialist support

6. Communication between early years teachers

7. Understanding and recognition of the needs of four year olds at every level

8. Space

9. Parental involvement

10. Non-contact time

11. Closer liaison with preschool organisations

3. There was still a lack of awareness of the fundamental importance of *involving parents* in the educational process and a lack of the required skills to manage successfully the many adults who interact with a child.

4. Many classrooms were overcrowded and lacking *appropriate and essential facilities and equipment*; factors which have an immediate effect on the quality of education experienced.

5. Other negative outcomes of the under resourcing of this first year in school were the *low status* ascribed to the work and the consequent loss of self confidence and self esteem. Morale is not just at the mercy of material conditions but improvements might do something to help teachers with their sense of professional underachievement.

6. There is still uncertainty about what constitutes an *appropriate curriculum* for these four year olds and little support at school and LEA level to guide here. Clear principles, priorities and rationales for practice were general-

ly lacking, which meant that teachers often felt undue pressure from outside sources. The gap between rhetoric and practice was often enormous.

7. The whole question of *whether four years olds should be in infant schools* at all was seen as a widely contentious issue. The range of opinions is exemplified below:

'Many four year old children are still very emotionally and physically immature when they begin school and with the best will in the world a busy reception class teacher cannot offer them the special attention that they would receive in a nursery class or school. The authority is fortunate in having many such nurseries and this system of an earlier start to school has disrupted what was far more beneficial to these young children. Parents are worried that their child may be without a school place unless they start, instead of a more satisfactory development from part time to full time nursery then to school when a child is truly ready.'

'I feel very strongly that the best person to educate a four year old is the mother and the best place is at home.'

'In view of the fact that children of four and five are learning at such a high rate I think it very important that they start school as early as possible.'

'Having operated the system for three years I am not convinced they should be in primary schools. I feel that very young children are expected to join in too quickly into infant/junior school life.'

'I would like to express my total support for the education of four year olds and the belief that every child should have the right to three full years of infant education. There are concerns however with regard to the quality of what is provided and its appropriateness to the needs of four year olds.'

'A properly designed and staffed nursery unit attached to the school would be far more beneficial to the needs of four year olds than integrating them into mainstream school so soon.'

Discussion

There are marked changes taking place in the pattern of admissions to school. Current figures show that over 60% of four year olds are in infant schools and that this figure is rising (DES 1989). This trend has been accompanied by the growing dismay of those who believe nursery education is the right form of provision for these young children; a view that has been supported by HMI (1989) and DES (1985) who have cast doubts on the ability of schools to deliver an appropriate curriculum unless it is adequately resourced. There is now a growing body of research which has looked at the quality of provision and endorses these warnings.

Bennett and Kell's (1989) study of practice in three local authorities confirms the finding that many teachers of four year olds are not trained for this age group and that resourcing in terms of equipment, materials, space and staff is often inadequate. They also pointed to the gap that exists between the rhetoric of many of these teachers and their practice. In discussion, teachers prioritised affective development and the importance of play but classroom practice was found to be dominated by formal teaching methods directed largely at children's cognitive development. The study goes on to argue that these factors have a direct effect on the quality and appropriateness of children's learning experiences. Bennett and Kell identify 'teaching problems' which included:

> poor specification of the purpose of activities, low expectations, poor matching, inadequate monitoring and a neglect of assessment and diagnosis. (p.76)

There are many questions raised by this study, some aspects of which call for alternative methods of investigation and analysis, but what remains clear is that infant schools need to examine their provision for four year olds critically and urgently. The current NFER research project entitled *The Educational Needs of Four Year Olds* which is a large scale national investigation, the results of which are due to be published early in 1990, should also provide much needed practical guidance for all those concerned with the education of four year olds.

It is evident that the policy of admitting four year olds into infant schools is likely to remain with us for the foreseeable future. Demographic changes resulting in a rising birth rate and an increasing need for mothers to return to work make the policy politically and economically attractive. Given this context, educators of these young children must be clear and vociferous in their demands for provision for four year olds to be of the highest quality. Meeting these demands will require a marked change in attitude at local and central level in order to provide teachers of four year olds with the training, support staff, facilities, equipment, space and guidance that are essential if the experience of starting school at four is to be a beneficial one for the child.

The evidence presented in this study seems to encapsulate a mix of hope and horror. The education of under fives is at last being given the attention it has been clamouring for and there are indications of positive responses being made to many of the concerns and issues discussed in this report. However, there is also evidence of teachers struggling against almost impossible demands and having to cope with little support in material or human terms. It is fatally easy for words to stay on a page; translating them into action or change is far more difficult. Yet the debate needs to be kept alive, and to be constructive and challenging. Building up our knowledge of the quality of the experience offered to four year olds in infant schools can only add to the understanding which is vital if we are to move from description to action. The following proposals for action are an attempt to provide some practical guidelines for those who wish to make a start:

— The provision of clear curriculum guidance from central government and LEAs.

— The appointment of more early years advisers and support staff.

— An expansion of inservice opportunities for teachers of four year olds and also headteachers and support staff.

— The development of local support groups and networks to facilitate exchange of ideas and information.

— A clear statement of policy that part time attendance is the norm for pre-statutory age children in infant schools.

— A requirement that teachers of four year old children should have received some form of appropriate training.

— Centrally prescribed minimum requirements for schools admitting four year olds which are comparable to those found in nursery schools and classes.

Address for correspondence:
Dr. Christine Pascal
Worcester College of Higher Education
Henwick Grove
Worcester
WR2 6AJ
United Kingdom

References

Barrett, G. (1986) Starting School: An Evaluation of the Experience. CARE. University of East Anglia.

Bennett, N. and Kell, J. (1989) A Good Start? Four Year Olds in Infant Schools. Blackwell Education, Oxford.

Cleave, S., Jowett, S. and Bate, M. (1982) And So To School. NFER-Nelson, Windsor.

Cleave, S., Barker-Lunn, J. and Sharp C. (1985) 'Local education authority policy on admission to infant/first school'. Educational Research 27, pp.40-43.

Department of Education and Science (1985) 'Better Schools'. Education White Paper, Cmnd. 9469. London, HMSO.

Department of Education and Science (1987) 'Pupil-teacher ratios for each Local Education Authority. January 1986'. Statistical Bulletin 8/87. London, HMSO.

Department of Education and Science (1989) 'Pupils under five years in each local education authority in England — January 1988'. Statistical Bulletin 7/89. London, HMSO.

Her Majesty's Inspectorate (1989) The Education of Children Under Five. London, HMSO.

House of Commons (1986) 'Achievement in Primary Schools', Report of the Select Committee on Education, Science and the Arts. London, HMSO.

House of Commons (1988) 'Educational Provision for the Under Fives Vols. 1 & 2, Report of the Education, Science and Arts Committee. London, HMSO.

Osborn, A.F. and Milbank, J.E. (1987) The Effects of Early Education. Oxford, Clarendon Press.

Pascal, C. and Ghaye, A. (1988) 'Four year old children in reception classrooms: participant perceptions and practice', Educational Studies Vol. 14, No. 2, pp.187-208.

Pascal, C. (1989) 'The odyssey of Beatrice; a case study of a four year old's introduction to infant school', in Working With Under Fives Training Pack. Milton Keynes, Open University Press.

Peel, J. (1988) 'The admission of four year old children to primary schools in Lancashire'. Paper presented to NFER Conference on Starting School at Four: Planning for the Future, Solihull.

Preschool Playgroups Association (1983) Easing the Transition from Home to School. Newcastle: Northern Region PPA.

Schweinhart, L.J., Weikart, D.P. and Larner, M.B. (1986) 'Consequences of three preschool curriculum models through age 15', Early Childhood Research Quarterly, 1 (1), pp.15-45.

Times Educational Supplement, 9th September 1988 'DES shelves disturbing survey on primary staffing', p.1.

Thomas, I. (1987) 'The Bedfordshire 4+ pilot scheme; some issues and implications', in NFER/SCDE Four Year Olds in School. Windsor, NFER.

Tizard, B., Blatchford, P., Burke, J., Farquhar, C. and Plewis, I. (1988) Young Children at School in the Inner City. London, Erlbaum Ass.

Woodhead, M. (1989) 'School starts at 5 . . . or 4 years old? The rationale for changing admission policy in England and Wales', Journal of Education Policy, 4, pp.1-22.